Great Bible Stories
MOSES
Fun Pad

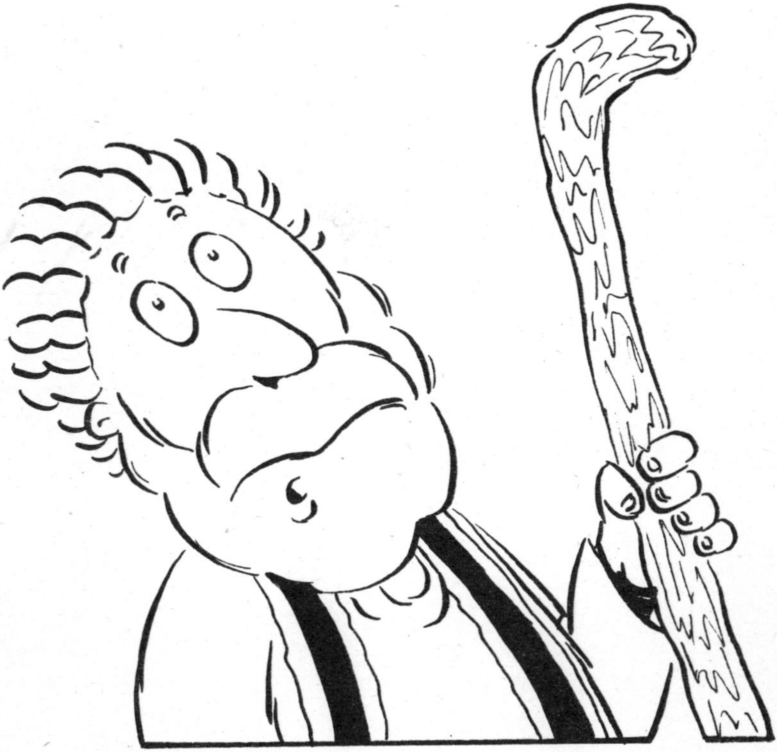

developed by Greg Holder
illustrated by Andy Stiles

David Match-Up

David loved to talk to God. Find two pictures of David praying that are the same.

Connect the Dots

What was baby Moses' hiding place?

How Many Sheep?

One of David's most-loved songs is Psalm 23. It tells us that God takes cares of us like a shepherd takes care of his sheep. How many sheep do you see?

Answer: 6

Mystery Maze

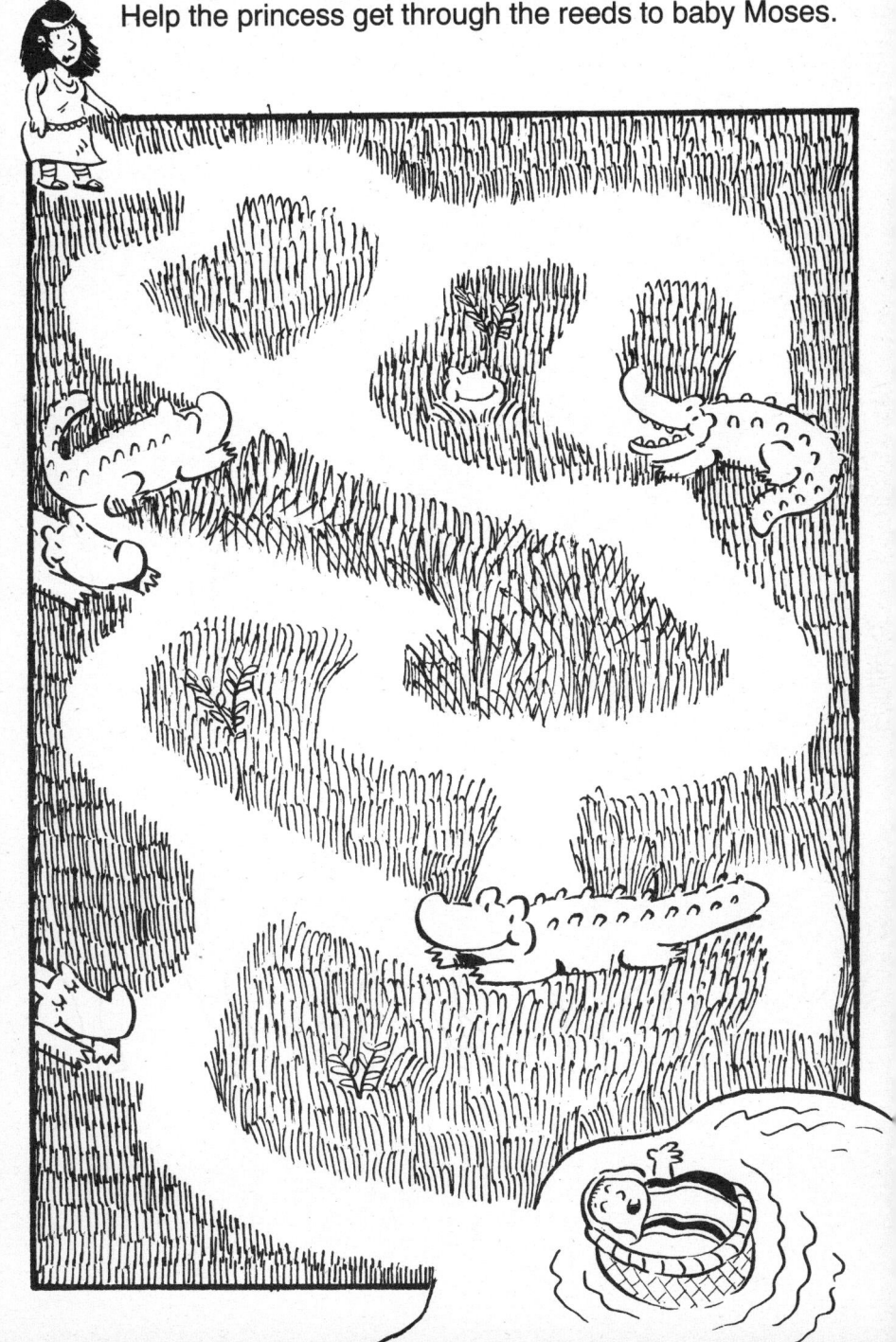

Where is the sound of crying come from?
Help the princess get through the reeds to baby Moses.

Musical Praise

David loved to write songs and poems to God. Use the code to find out which book of the Bible is full of David's songs.

__ __ __ __ __ __
4 5 2 3 1 5

Answer: Psalms

Which One?

The princess asked Moses' mother to take care of him until he was old enough to live at the palace. Find the baby that is different from all the others.

Color by Number

After Saul died, David became king of Israel.
Use the code to color the picture.

1=PURPLE   2=YELLOW   3=BROWN   4=RED   5=BLUE

What's Wrong Here?

Moses grew up in the palace of the king of Egypt. Find five things that are wrong in this picture.

Straight As an Arrow

Jonathan shot an arrow as a message for David. Help Jonathan's arrow get through the maze so David will know the message.

Picture Search

Moses saw that his people, the Hebrews, had to work very hard in Egypt. Find these tools in the box in the order as below. Look up, down, and across.

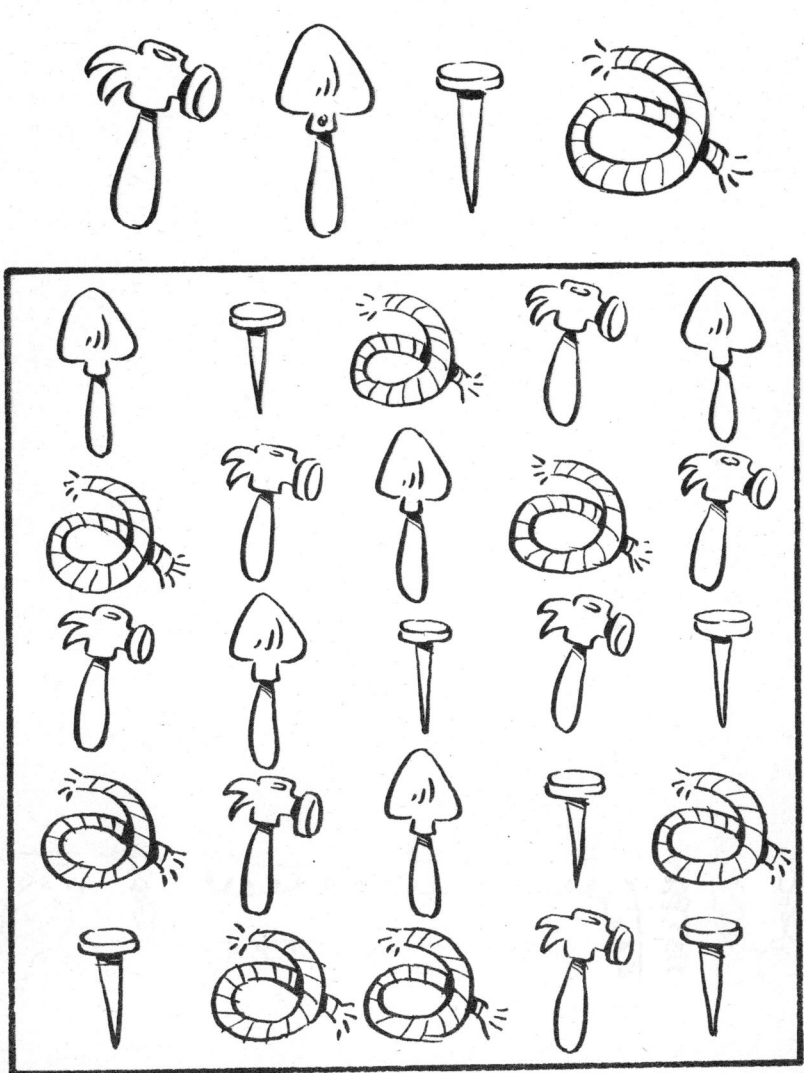

Follow the Dots

King Saul became jealous of David and tried to hurt him. Where did David hide?

Color by Number

In the desert, God spoke to Moses from a burning bush. Color this picture using the color code.

1=BROWN 2=GREEN 3=BLUE
4=YELLOW 5=RED 6=TAN

What's Different?

With God's help, David defeated the mighty Goliath. Find five things that are different in these two pictures.

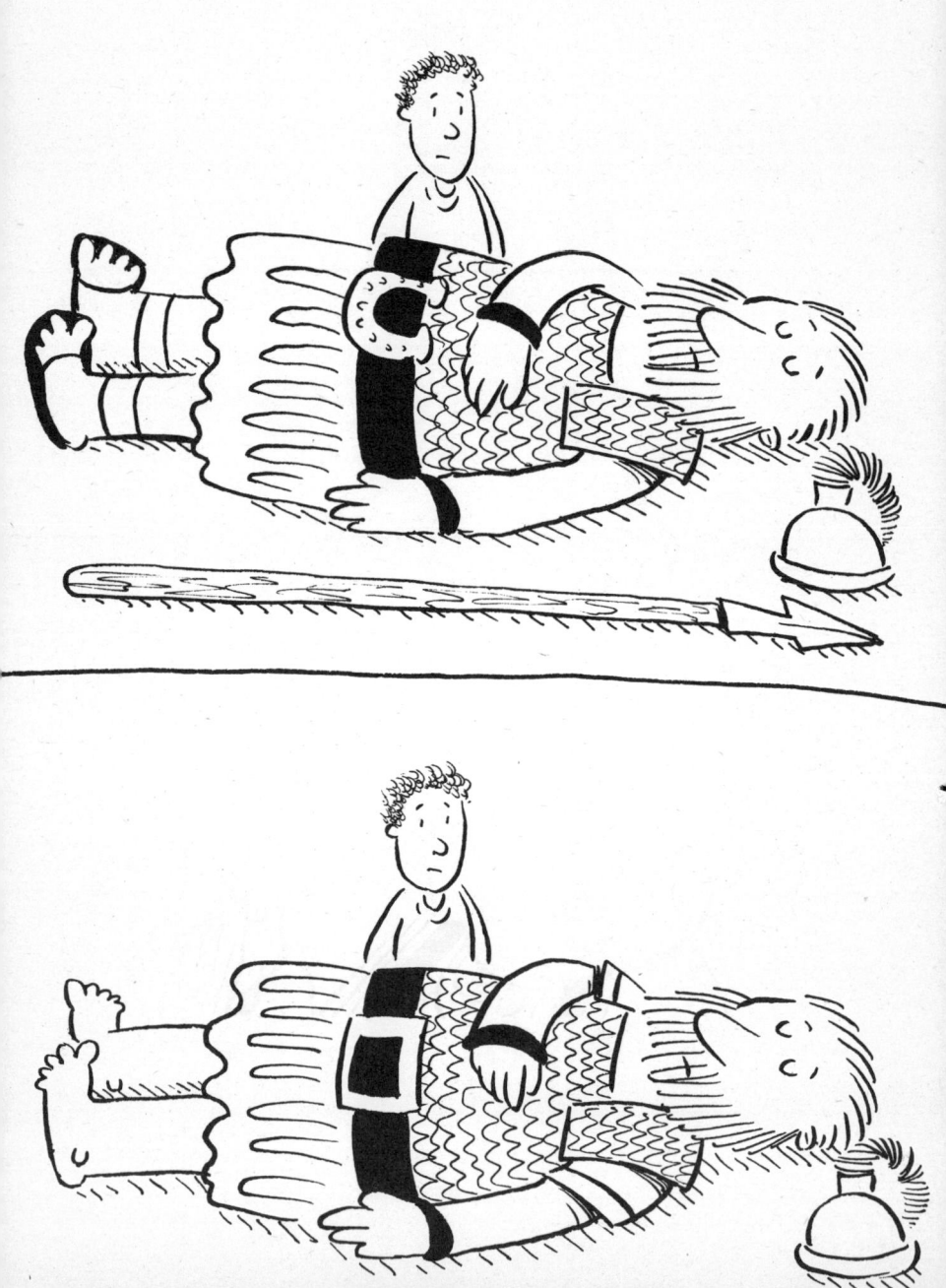

Unscramble the Message

What did God tell Moses to do?

_____ ___ _____
NRIGB   YM   OPLEEP

_____ ___ _____.
UOT   FO   YGPET.

Answer: Bring my people out of Egypt.

Search the Picture

David went to fight Goliath with only a sling and five smooth stones. **Sling** and **stone** begin with the letter **S**. Circle everything in the picture that begins with **S**.

Desert Daze

Moses' brother Aaron went to Egypt with Moses. Help them find their way through the desert.

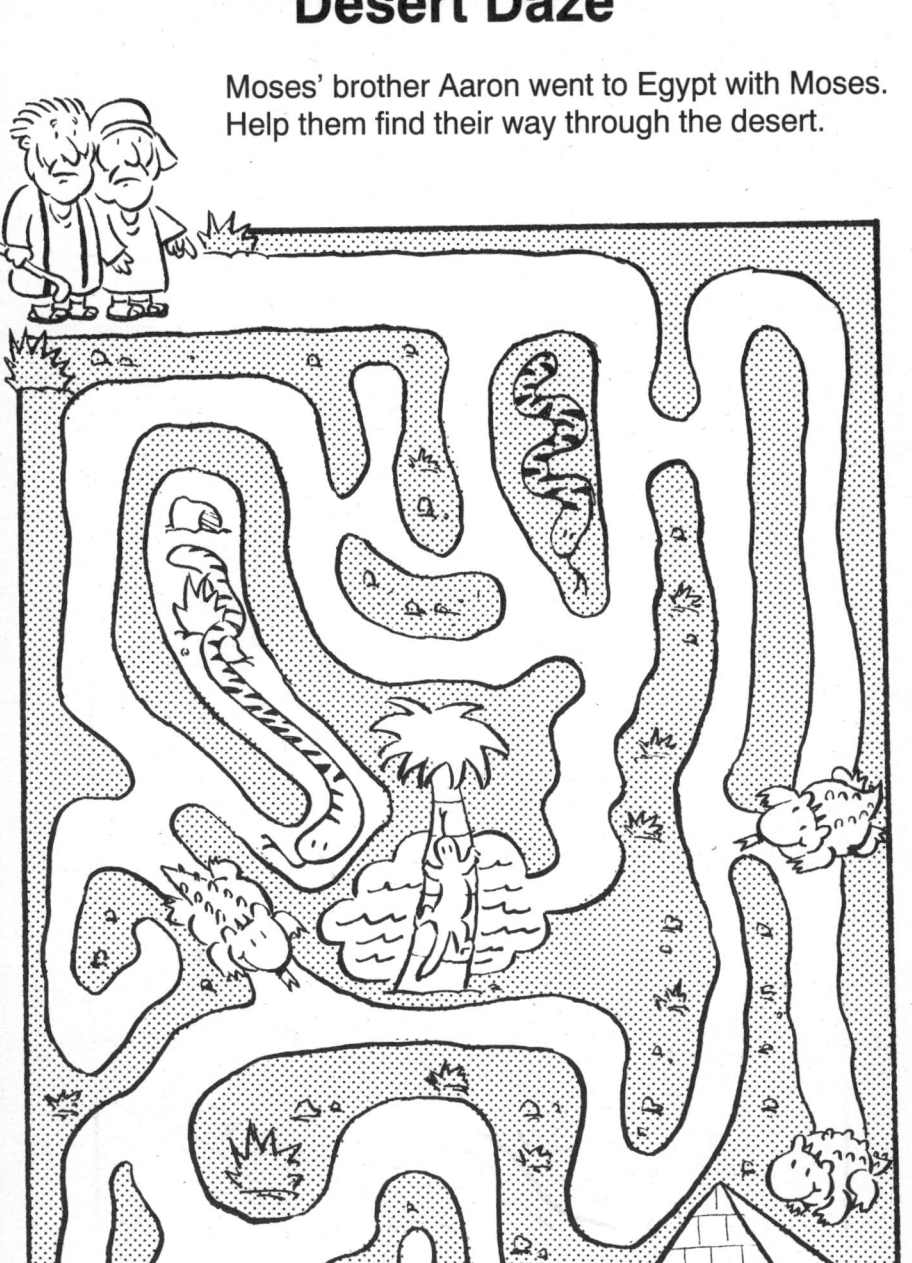

Warrior Word Search

Goliath the giant was a mighty Philistine soldier. Find these five things that Goliath carried with him into battle.

SWORD SHIELD ARMOR
HELMET SPEAR

Color the Picture

God parted the Red Sea so Moses and the Israelites could escape from the Egyptians.

What's Wrong Here?

David often played his harp for King Saul.
Circle the six things that are wrong in this picture.

Connect the Dots

When the Israelites were safe, Moses' sister Miriam praised God with a song and dancing. What instrument did Miriam play?

Samuel Match-Up

The prophet Samuel said that David would one day become king of Israel. Which two pictures of Samuel are exactly alike?

Count the Quail

In the wilderness, God sent quail for the Israelites to eat. How many quail do you see?

Answer: 5

How Many Brothers?

Hidden in the puzzle is the number of David's brothers. Find the number and color it.

Draw and Color

During the daytime, God led Moses and the Israelites with a giant pillar of cloud. Draw the pillar of cloud. Then color the picture.

Connect the Dots

What instrument did David play?

Moses Match-Up

God gave Moses the Ten Commandments on two stone tablets. Match the picture to the correct shadow.

Finish the Picture

Once, David had to fight a lion to save his sheep. Use the dotted lines and the squares below to finish the other half of this lion.

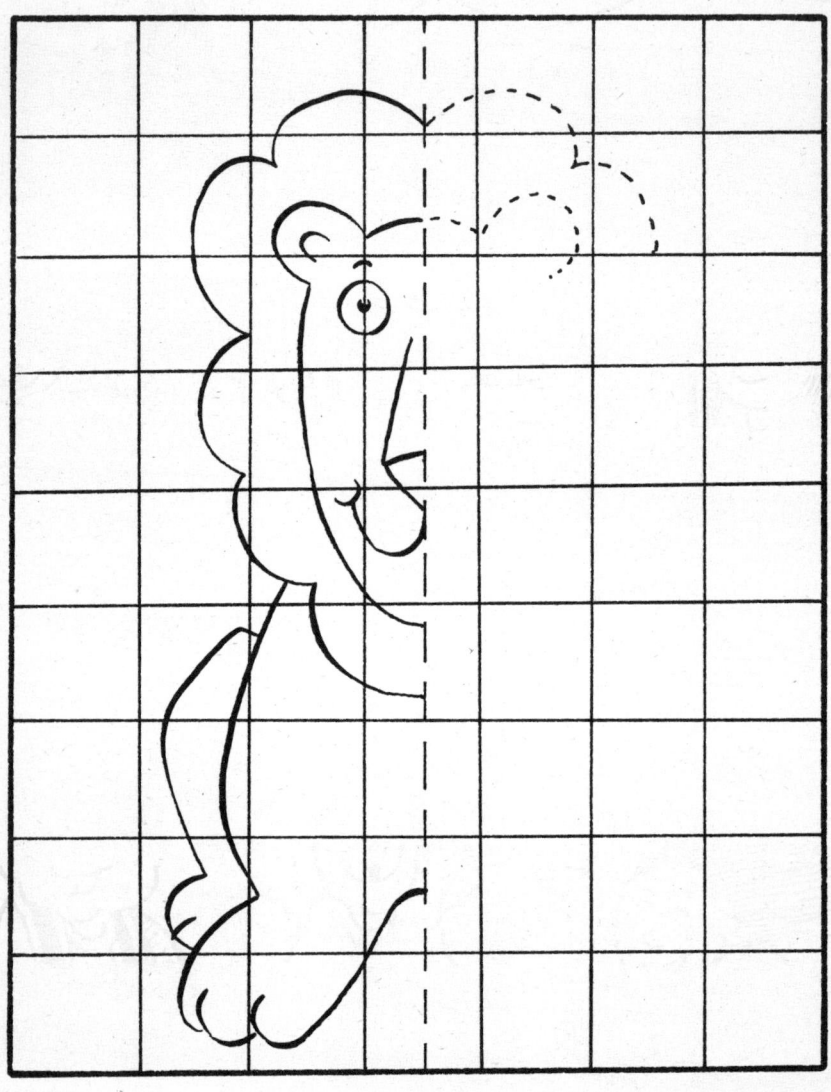

Find Six

God made water come out of a rock for the Israelites to drink. Find six things that don't belong in this picture.

Find David's Lost Sheep

When David was a young, he was a shepherd. Help David find his lost lamb.

Do You Know?

Unscramble these words to see how old Moses lived to be.

NEO   DHDUENR   NDA   NTYWTE

___ _____ ___ _____

Answer: One hundred and twenty

Great Bible Stories
DAVID
Fun Pad

developed by Greg Holder
illustrated by Andy Stiles